THINGS IN THE KITCHEN

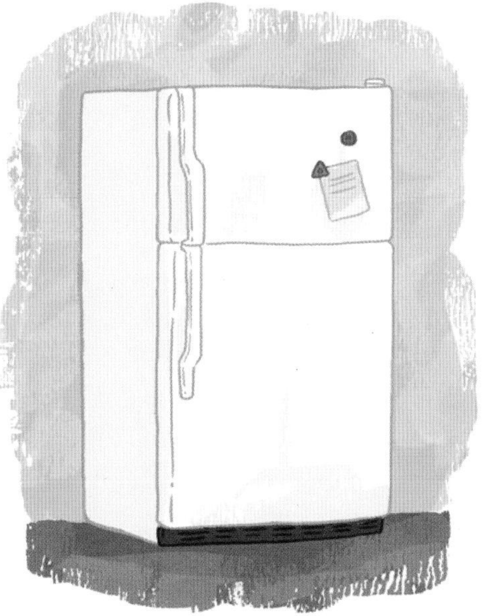

ILLUSTRATED BY

Ali Hinch

This is a stove.

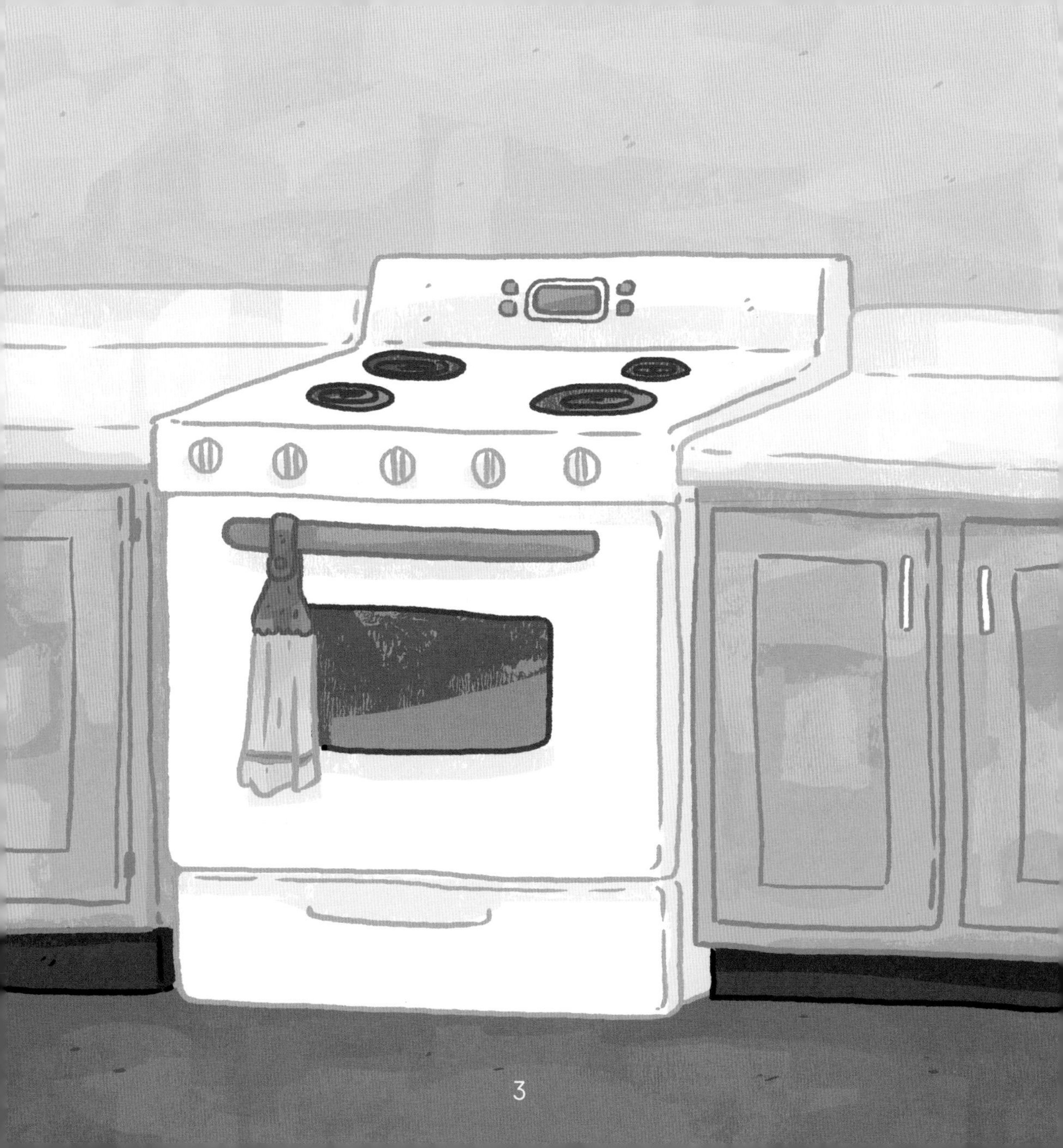

This is a fridge.

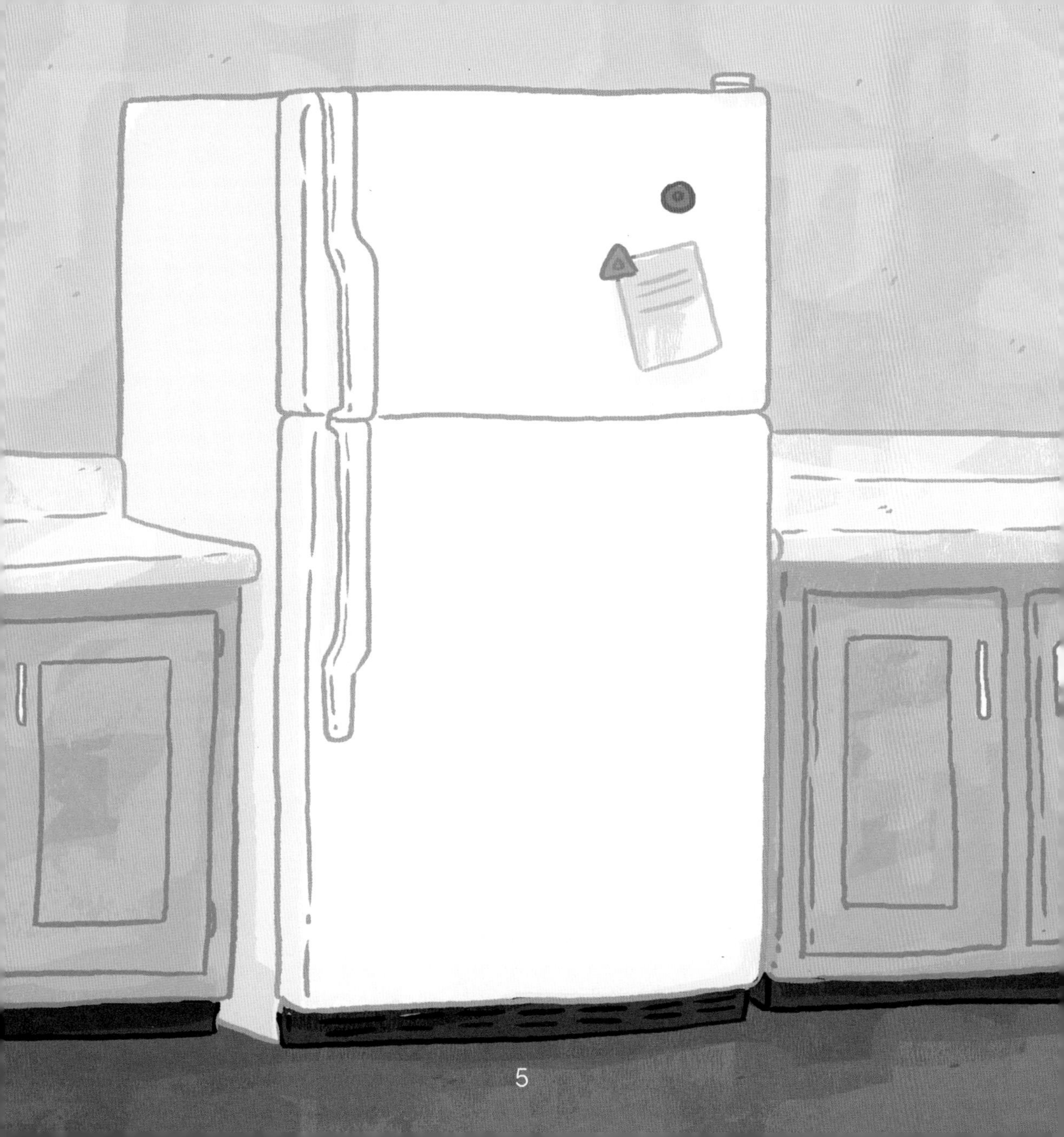

This is a clock.

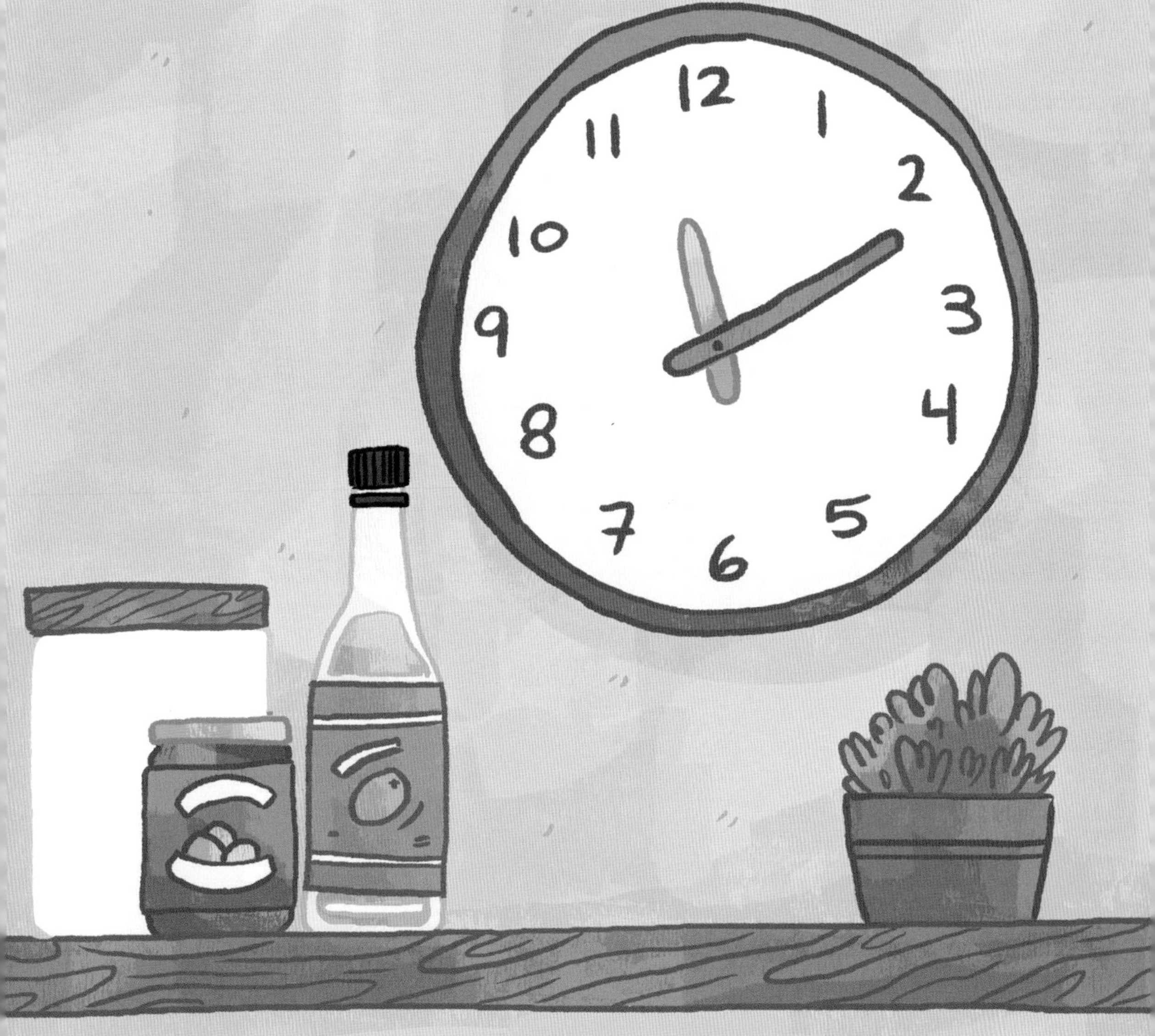
12
1
2
3
4
5
6
7
8
9
10
11

This is a sink.

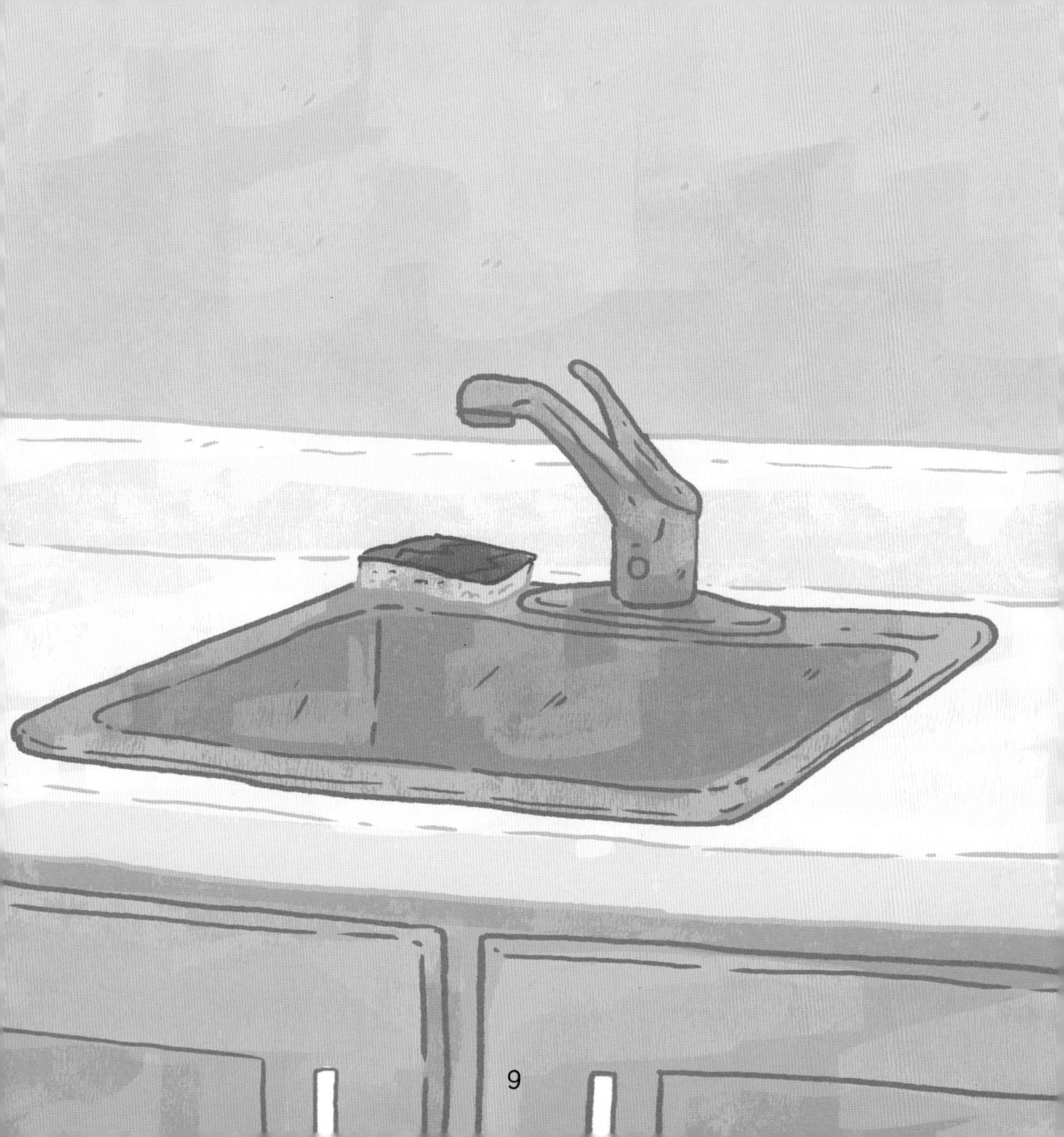

This is a cupboard.

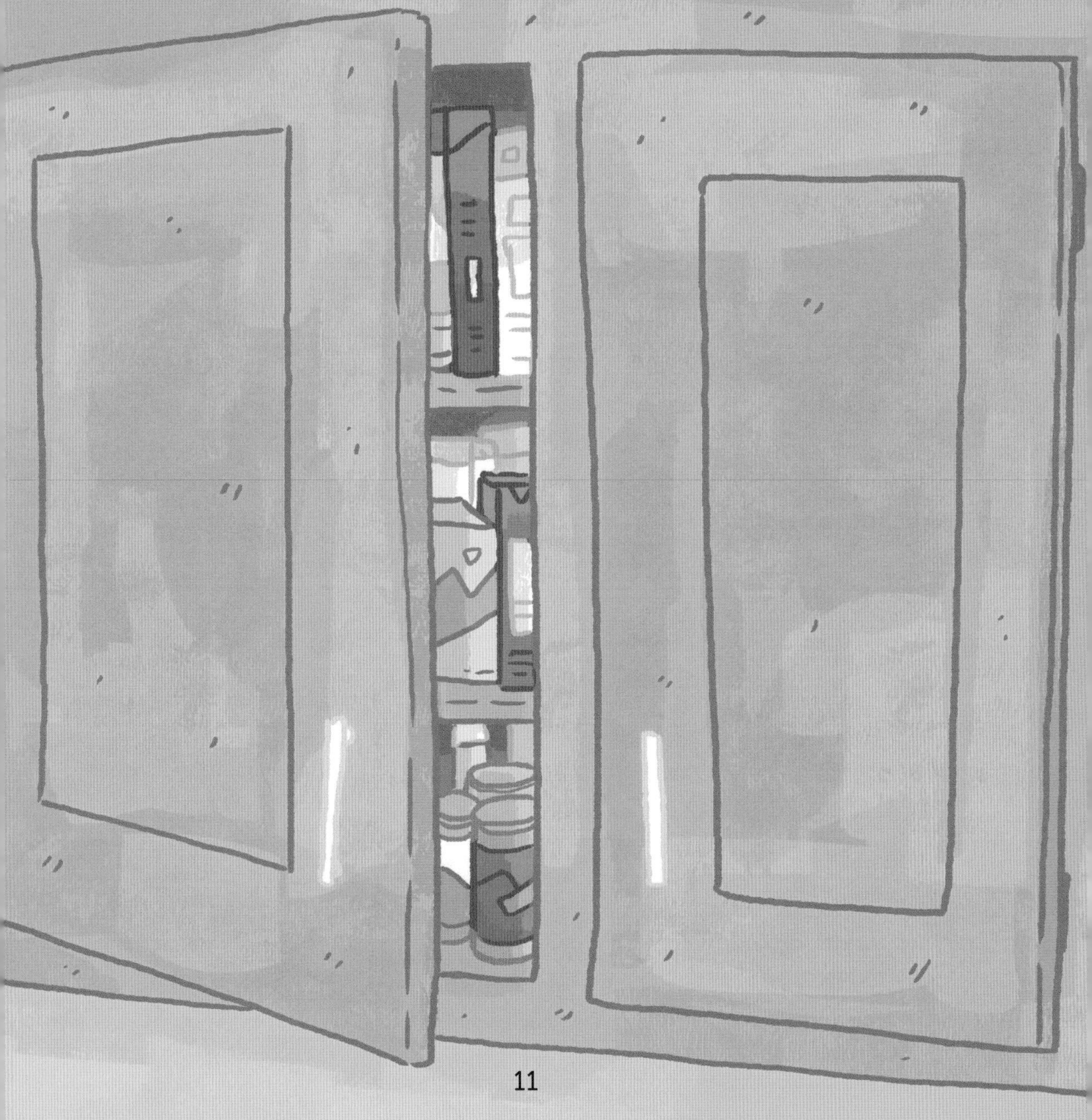

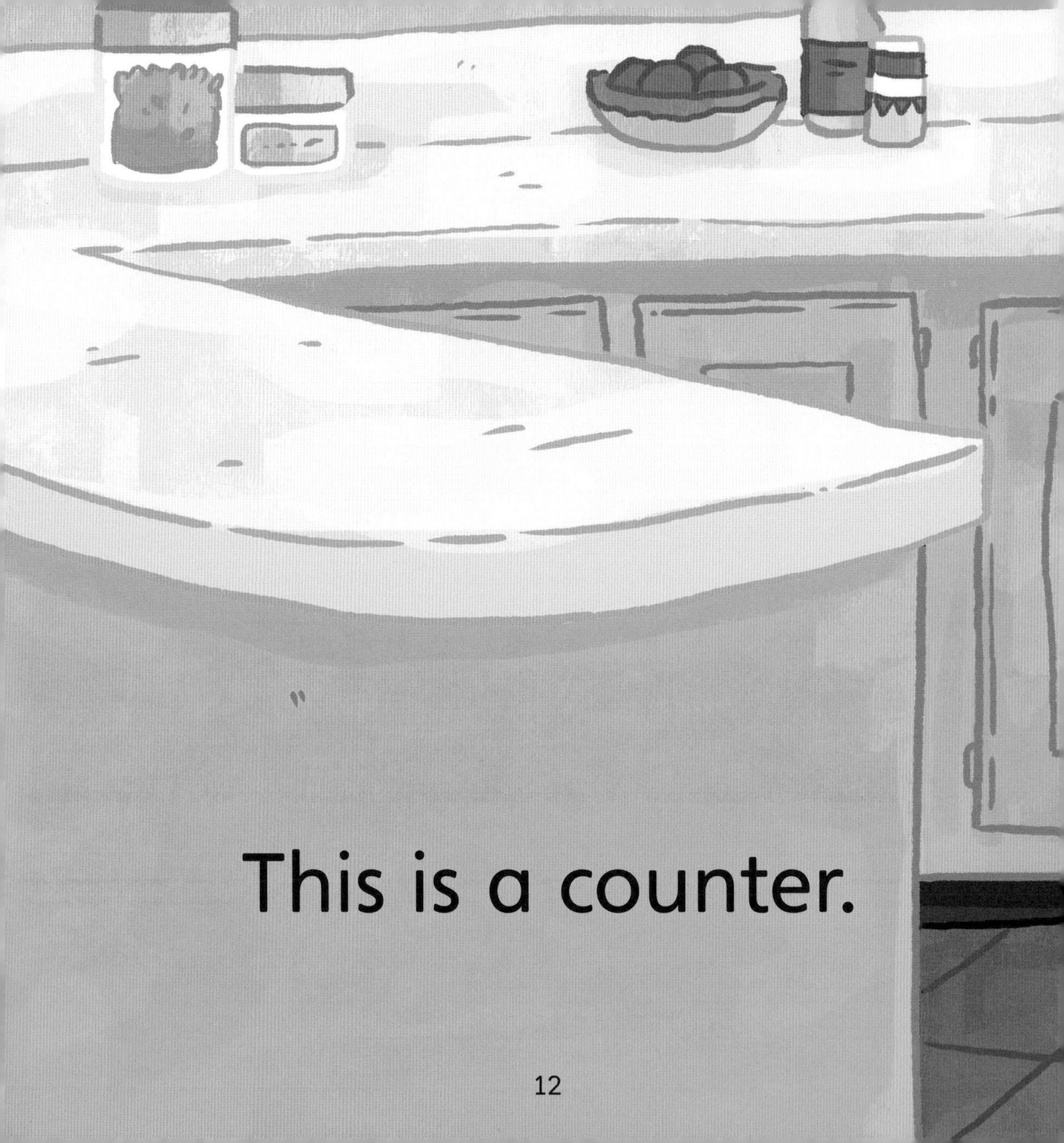

This is a counter.